Contents

Some words are shown in bold, **like this**. You can find out what they mean by looking in the glossary.

Do you want a pet hamster?

Hi! I'm Nibble the hamster, and I'm very happy to meet you. Did you know that hamsters like me make great pets? We're clean, friendly, and quite easy to look after. We're also fun to keep.

PETS' GUIDES

Nibble's Guide to

Caring for Your Hamster

Anita Ganeri

Raintree

Raintree is an imprint of Capstone Global Library Limited, a company incorporated in England and Wales having its registered office at 7 Pilgrim Street, London, EC4V 6LB – Registered company number: 6695582

To contact Raintree:
Phone: 0845 6044371
Fax: + 44 (0) 1865 312263
Email: myorders@raintreepublishers.co.uk
Outside the UK please telephone +44 1865 312262

Edited by Daniel Nunn, Rebecca Rissman, and Sian Smith
Designed by Cynthia Della-Rovere
Picture research by Tracy Cummins
Original illustrations © Capstone Global Library Ltd 2013
Illustrated by Rick Peterson
Production by Victoria Fitzgerald
Originated by Capstone Global Library Ltd
Printed and bound in China by South China Printing Company Ltd

ISBN 978 1 4062 5060 2 (hardback)
16 15 14 13 12
10 9 8 7 6 5 4 3 2 1

ISBN 978 1 4062 5067 1 (paperback)
17 16 15 14 13
10 9 8 7 6 5 4 3 2 1

British Library Cataloguing in Publication Data
Ganeri, Anita, 1961-
   Nibble's guide to caring for your hamster. – (Pets' guides)
   1. Hamsters as pets–Juvenile literature.
   I. Title II. Series
   636.9'356-dc23

Acknowledgements
The author and publisher are grateful to the following for permission to reproduce copyright material: Alamy pp. 13 (© Top-Pet-Pics), 21 (© Papilio), 23 (© Top-Pet-Pics); Biosphoto p. 5 (Michel Gunther); Capstone Library pp. 7, 11, 15, 17, 25 (Karon Dubke); iStockphoto pp. 19 (© Daniel Juhl Mogensen), 27 (© Andres Balcazar); Shutterstock p. 9 (© Victoria Rak @Tuff Photo).

Cover photograph of a black-bellied hamster reproduced with permission of Superstock (© age fotostock). Design elements reproduced with permission of Shutterstock (© Picsfive) and Shutterstock (© R-studio).

We would like to thank Teresa Linford (Mad About Hamsters) for her assistance in the preparation of this book.

Every effort has been made to contact copyright holders of material reproduced in this book. Any omissions will be rectified in subsequent printings if notice is given to the publisher.

You'll need to be a good pet owner and look after me properly. I'll need food, water, and a clean, safe place to live in. Then I'll quickly become your best friend.

Choosing your hamster

There are lots of different types of hamster you can choose from. I'm a golden hamster. I get my name from the colour of my fur. Golden hamsters like me are happy living on our own. We don't like living with other hamsters.

These hamsters are babies and will soon need to live alone.

You can buy a hamster from a pet shop or go to an animal shelter. Animal shelters often have hamsters that need good, new homes.

A healthy hamster

Pick a hamster that looks happy and healthy, just like me! Look at my round body, soft, shiny fur, and bright, clear eyes. I'm your perfect pet!

Your new pet should be lively and nosy. I'm always scurrying about. A hamster that's scared or crouching in a corner may not be very well.

Getting ready

Before you bring me home, there are a few things that you need to get ready. Here is my hamster home-coming shopping list…

Nibble's shopping list

 a large cage with a **nest box**

shredded tissue paper or hay for bedding

wood shavings for the floor of the cage

an exercise wheel

a **drip-feeder** water bottle

a food bowl

hamster food.

My new home

Like all hamsters, I love climbing and running about. Please make sure that you get me a big cage with plenty of room and a cosy **nest box** for sleeping in.

Put my cage somewhere safe and warm, but out of bright sunlight and away from chilly **draughts**. Make sure that the door closes properly. I'm brilliant at escaping!

Coming home

You can carry me home in a small cardboard box with holes in so that I can breathe. At home, put me in my cage. I might be shy at first so leave me alone for a few hours to settle in.

Give me a gentle stroke at first so that I get used to being **handled**. Later, you can pick me up by scooping me up gently in both hands. Let me climb from one of your hands to the other. Talk to me softly so that I don't feel frightened.

Dinner time

It's dinner time and I'm hungry! I like to have one meal a day, in the evening. Don't worry if I store some of my food in the **pouches** in my cheeks. I'm saving it to eat later!

Nibble the Hamster's top meal-time tips

- Feed me a mixture of seeds, nuts, and **grains**. You can buy special hamster food from a pet shop.

- Put my food in a heavy dish so that it doesn't tip over.

- Keep my water bottle topped up with fresh water.

Time for play

Hamsters like me need lots of exercise and chances to play. Otherwise, we quickly get bored and unhappy. Cardboard tubes and glass jars make great hamster toys.

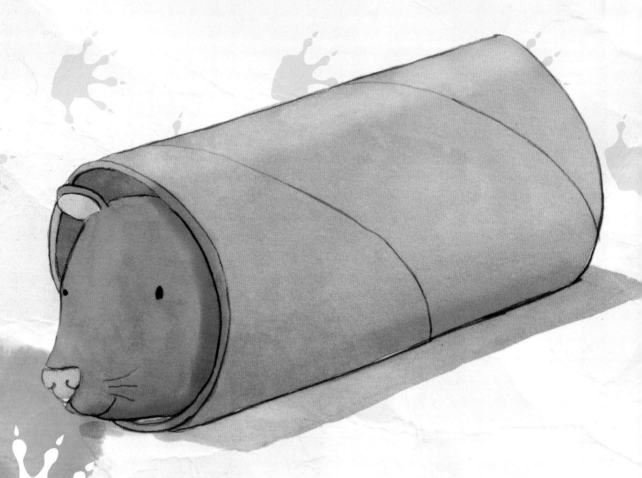

You can also put an exercise wheel in my cage. Make sure that it's solid so I don't get my feet trapped. Then I can go for a run at night – that's when I'm wide awake.

Cleaning my cage

Please keep my cage nice and clean. Otherwise, I might get ill. Every day, take away any **droppings** and bits of old food. Wash out my food bowl and water bottle.

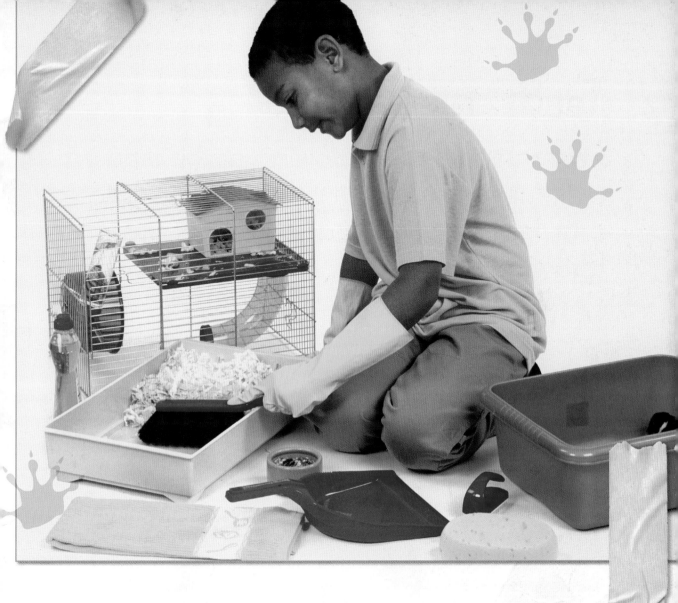

Once a week, you need to clean my whole cage out. Put fresh bedding in my **nest box** and fresh wood shavings on the floor. Don't forget to wash your hands afterwards.

Teeth and fur

My front teeth keep growing all the time. I'm quite used to that. But if they get too long, I can't eat properly. Please give me a wooden **gnawing** block to wear my teeth down.

You can groom your hamster with its own soft toothbrush.

I've got short fur so I can **groom** it with my front paws to keep it clean and glossy. If you've got a long-haired hamster, you need to groom it every other day with a soft brush.

Visiting the vet

Hamsters like me will stay fit and healthy if you take good care of us. If I don't look well, take me to the vet. Just like you, I can catch colds and flu – AAATCHOOO!

There are other signs that show you that I'm not feeling very well. Take me to the vet if my breathing sounds noisy, my eyes are cloudy, my bottom is dirty, or if I go off my food.

Holiday care

Don't just go away and leave me when you go on holiday. I still need food, fresh water, and clean bedding, so ask a friend or neighbour to look after me.

Take me to a friend's house or tell them to call in every day. It's a good idea to leave plenty of supplies and a list of what they need to do. Then they won't forget anything.

Hamster facts

- Wild hamsters live in the desert. They sleep in **burrows** that they dig deep underground. This helps to keep them cool.

- Wild hamsters eat a mixture of seeds, **grains**, insects such as crickets, and baby insects.

- Hamsters cannot see very well. They use their whiskers to help them find their way around.

- Hamsters usually live for about two years, though some can live for longer.

Helpful tips

- Use wood shavings instead of sawdust in your hamster's cage. Sawdust is very fine and may irritate your hamster's nose.

- Every few days, give your hamster a tiny piece of fruit or vegetable as a treat. Don't feed your hamster oranges, lemons, onions, grapes, or rhubarb.

- A good way of letting your hamster get to know you is to sit in a dry bath. Then let your hamster climb over you.

- Never leave your hamster alone with another animal, even if they seem like good friends. They might frighten or harm your hamster.

Glossary

burrows holes that hamsters and other animals dig in the ground to live in

draughts blasts of cold air that come through windows or under doors

drip-feeder a bottle that is fixed to a hamster's cage and lets water slowly drip out

droppings hamster poo

gnawing a way of chewing and biting

grains food such as corn or wheat that comes from plants

groom to brush and clean a hamster's fur. Hamsters also groom their own fur.

handled when a hamster is picked up and stroked

nest box a box that is filled with soft bedding for a hamster to sleep in

pouches spaces inside a hamster's cheeks where it stores pieces of food

shredded paper that has been torn into lots of small pieces

Find out more

Books to read

Gerbils and Hamsters (Pets Plus), Sally Morgan (Franklin Watts, 2012)

Hamster (Collins Family Pet Guide), David Alderton (Collins, 2011)

Websites

www.hamsters-uk.org

The National Hamster Council in the UK gives you information about keeping, caring for, and showing hamsters.

www.rspca.org.uk

Visit the Royal Society for the Prevention of Cruelty to Animals website to find out lots of information about pet care.

Index